578840

MODERN COMMUNICATIONS

*The London Post Office
Tower under construction*

MODERN
COMMUNICATIONS

written and illustrated by CHARLES KING

TRICORNE
BOOKS

GEORGE G. HARRAP & CO. LTD
LONDON   TORONTO   WELLINGTON   SYDNEY

First published in Great Britain 1970
by GEORGE G. HARRAP & CO. LTD
182 High Holborn, London W.C.1

Hardback SBN 245 59836 7
Limp edition SBN 245 59976 2

Filmset by Keyspools Ltd, Golborne, Lancs
Printed by C. Tinling & Co. Ltd, London and Prescot
Made in Great Britain

CONTENTS

	page
THE POST OFFICE TOWER	7
Why the Tower was necessary	8
How the Tower was built	10
The cable chamber	12
Incoming telephone calls	13
Television control room	14
Ventilation and refrigeration equipment	16
Telephony transmission equipment	16
Battery room	16
Waveguide pressurization room—Aerials	17
Restaurant—Lifts—Radar	17
Maintenance	18
World-wide development of microwaves	20
Telecommunications	23
CABLES	24
Overhead cables	24
Underground cables	26
Pressurization of underground cables	28
Repeaters	28
Submarine cables	29
Cable ships	32
TELEPHONES	35
The Exchange a Manual	37
b Automatic	38
Dialling tones	39
Subscriber trunk dialling—STD	41
The speaking clock service—TIM	41
All figures by 1970	42

CONTENTS *(continued)*

	page
TELEGRAMS	43
TELEX—talking by typewriter	44
DATEL—data by telephone	46
RADIO	47
'Ship to shore' service	47
SATELLITES	49
'Echo'—'Score'	51
'Telstar'	52
'Relay'	53
'Syncom'	54
Tracking stations	56
INTO THE FUTURE	59
ACKNOWLEDGMENTS	62
INDEX	63

THE POST OFFICE TOWER

The great shining column of the Post Office Tower rises like a giant lighthouse from the vast sea of buildings that is London. From this sea, which is as wide and broad as the eye can reach, rise other tall buildings of steel and concrete into the clear air, but none so tall as the Tower. With its height of 620 feet (189 metres), it is the tallest building in Britain, and over 13,000 tons of steel, concrete and glass have gone into its construction. It is a triumph of engineering and modern architecture; slender and practical and packed with equipment, it represents the most advanced techniques in the history of modern communications.

The London Post Office Tower was officially opened by the Prime Minister on 8th October 1965. It was opened to the public on 19th May 1966

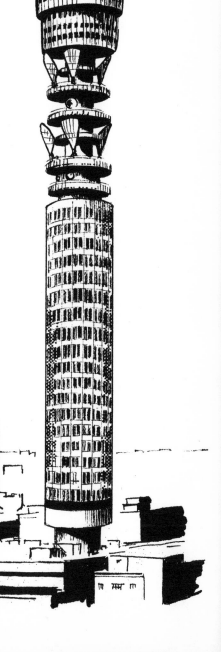

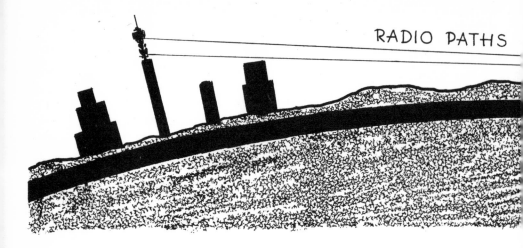

WHY THE TOWER WAS NECESSARY

The tower was not designed merely to be a showpiece of modern architecture. It is strictly functional, and there is a purpose in its great height. Why was it built? The main purpose was to provide more long distance telephone circuits and more television channels. In the past few years the demand for telecommunication services has stepped up tremendously. The telephone saves time and money and the number of local and trunk calls made is increasing steadily year by year. More and more people are buying or hiring television sets, which also presents problems for the Post Office. In addition, more channels have been required to extend the BBC 2 service, and to allow for the introduction of colour television.

All this could have been done in the old-fashioned way, ripping up the roads and pavements of London to lay many more new cables. But just think what this would have cost in time and money! Instead, the Post Office Tower provides an extra service in the form of microwave radio channels which carry the telephone calls and television programmes between London and every part of the British Isles through the air instead of under ground. It is easing the tremendous

Radio beams must be angled to clear tall buildings and hills. In this diagram the curvature of the earth has been greatly exaggerated

pressure on Britain's trunk telephone services, and will be able to absorb the ever increasing expansion for at least a generation ahead.

The Tower has justly been likened to a lighthouse, which sends out its beams in a straight line. A microwave beam travels, like light, in a straight line, and any obstacles in its path, such as tall buildings or trees, cause loss of signal power and distortion. The Tower's horn and dish aerials are placed high enough to allow the microwaves to clear the tallest office blocks and the hills which rise in the distant suburbs. London itself lies in a hollow, so that the Tower had to be built high enough to allow for this and to rise well above the existing buildings and those planned for the future. An agreement has been made between the GPO and the Greater London Council that no building will be allowed to interfere with the transmission and reception from the Tower. The microwaves travel for 25 to 30 miles before being picked up by another tower's aerial system at the next relay point. Here the waves have to be strengthened and redirected because of the earth's curve. (See diagram).

While still under construction, the tower's cantilevered floors were easily visible. The telephone kiosk in the foreground is a reminder of one of the tower's main functions

HOW THE TOWER WAS BUILT

You may have seen the top of a tall flagpole swaying and bending in a high wind. This happens with very slim tall buildings and radio masts, for the wind exerts enormous pressures. Normally, architects design their structures to withstand any wind pressure with perfect safety. A building as tall and slender as the Tower could be allowed to sway several feet without worrying the builders and architects. The Post Office Tower, however, had to be as rigid as possible, because its aerials have to be accurately in line with other stations. A scale model was made, and wind tunnel tests were carried out by the National Physical Laboratory. These tests showed that the suggested building methods would produce a tower that was both rigid enough and completely safe.

The Tower has been built with a hollow central shaft of reinforced concrete, from which the many floors are cantilevered like ribs on a spinal column. This shaft tapers as it rises and is anchored to the main buildings by a 'collar' to make it even more stable. Owing to this highly successful design, a 90 mile an hour gust of wind would cause a movement of only 15 inches at the top.

The tower is anchored to the main building by a 'collar' to make it even more stable in strong wind. Any movement of the tower would alter the angle of the radio beams

The 'Collar'

STORM WARNING RADAR

THE CABLE CHAMBER

There are many Post Office cable tunnels, some of them as much as seven feet in diameter, leading from telephone exchanges in the London area to the Tower. The thick grey lead-covered cables snake up from below through a round metal grating into the cable chamber where they are fixed to large steel racks.

In order to prevent water seeping through damaged parts of the lead-covered cables lying in wet ground, the G.P.O. have a method of pumping dry air into the cables under pressure. This air forces its way out through any cracks in the cable, thus preventing water from seeping in. In the cable chamber is an alarm system which sends out a warning signal if pressure inside the cables falls below a certain level.

Floor / Stage		
41	580 ft	
40		LIFT MOTORS
37–39	548 ft	LIFT EQUIPMENT
36		KITCHENS
35		COCKTAIL BAR
34		RESTAURANT
33		PUBLIC
32		OBSERVATION PLATFORMS
31	477 ft	
30		HORN · · · AERIALS
28		MICROWAVE · · · DISHES
27		HORN · · · AERIALS
25		MICROWAVE · · · DISHES
23	355 ft	WAVEGUIDE PRESSURIZATION
22		RADIO 11,000 MHz
21		" 6,000 MHz
20		" 4,000 MHz
19		BATTERIES
18		RADIO 2,000 MHz
17		OUTSIDE BROADCASTS
16		BASEBAND
15		CONTROL FOR
14		RADIO SYSTEMS
13		BATTERIES
12		TELEPHONY TRANSMISSION EQUIPMENT
11		
10		ADMINISTRATION
9		VENTILATION
8		"
7		"
6	115 ft	
5		REFRIGERATION PLANT

4	TOWER LINK – CABLE ENTRY – VENTILATION PLANT	4TH FLOOR
3	TELEVISION EQUIPMENT	3RD "
2	T.V. NETWORK SWITCHING CENTRE	2ND "
	MERCURY INCOMING – TANDEM – TRUNK TESTING	1ST "
1	MDF REPEATER STN MERCURY INCOMING	GROUND
	CABLE CHAMBER – BATTERIES – VENTILATION	BASEMENT
	DIESELS – POWER PLANT – FUEL	SUB-BASEMENT

Diagrammatic section of the Post Office Tower

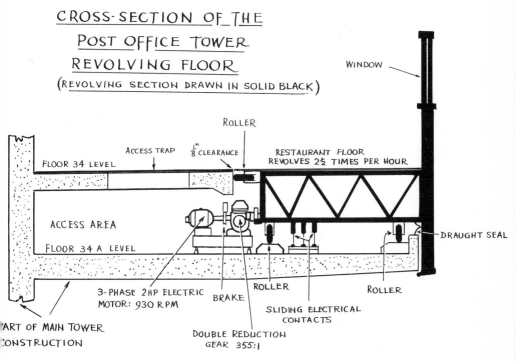

CROSS-SECTION OF THE POST OFFICE TOWER REVOLVING FLOOR
(REVOLVING SECTION DRAWN IN SOLID BLACK)

WINDOW

ROLLER

ACCESS TRAP — $\frac{1}{8}$" CLEARANCE

FLOOR 34 LEVEL

RESTAURANT FLOOR REVOLVES 2½ TIMES PER HOUR

ACCESS AREA

FLOOR 34 A LEVEL

DRAUGHT SEAL

3-PHASE 2HP ELECTRIC MOTOR: 930 RPM

BRAKE

ROLLER

ROLLER

SLIDING ELECTRICAL CONTACTS

PART OF MAIN TOWER CONSTRUCTION

DOUBLE REDUCTION GEAR 355:1

NOT DRAWN TO SCALE

INCOMING TELEPHONE CALLS

The Mercury Exchange receives calls made to London from the provinces and routes them to their destination in the London area.

In this department are also the trunk testing service, where technicians constantly test the lines for faults which they trace and put right immediately, and the Tandem exchange. This is an automatic telephone exchange which connects subscribers (the subscriber is the person making, and therefore paying for, the telephone call) with others on a different exchange in the London area.

The G.P.O. plays an important part in the country's television system. Signals are sent from the studio to the headquarters of the programme company and on to the Post Office Tower for switching to the transmitter. The signals are carried into towns and over distances less than 20 miles by underground cable, but for inter-city links these signals

Technicians sitting at the long banks of consoles in the TV Control Switching Room are responsible for switching programmes to the transmitter at exactly the right time

are routed over radio channels from the Tower, using the horn and dish aerials.

Great care has to be taken not to distort the very complicated signals, and engineers in the control room send special test signals over all circuits each day. They can also provide alternative routes if necessary.

While the B.B.C. send their signals over permanent circuits, the I.T.A. rent and control a network of inter-city radio links. Programme material is supplied by various companies, and it is the job of the man in the control room to switch the right programme to the transmitter at the right time. The actual switch is made by an electronic clock synchronised to TIM (see p. 41), and more than 5,000 switches a month are made here with no loss of programme time. In other words, viewers see the entire programme from start to finish and do not lose either the opening titles or the closing scenes.

On the floor above, the quality and strength of pictures being transmitted from the Tower are checked and controlled.

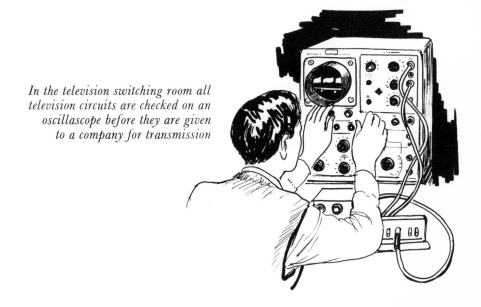

In the television switching room all television circuits are checked on an oscilloscope before they are given to a company for transmission

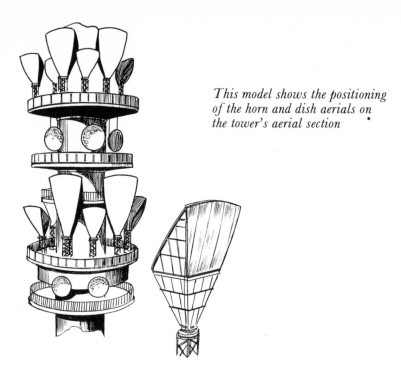

This model shows the positioning of the horn and dish aerials on the tower's aerial section •

VENTILATION AND REFRIGERATION EQUIPMENT

The equipment keeps the air in the entire Tower building at an even, comfortable temperature. The refrigeration plant cools the apparatus rooms which contain equipment that becomes heated.

TELEPHONY TRANSMISSION EQUIPMENT

This equipment translates normal spoken telephone signals into the much higher frequencies needed for transmission over the trunk cables or microwave paths. It also works the other way round, bringing high frequency signals into the audible range.

BATTERY ROOM

The batteries in this room serve the telephone switching equipment. The gravity of acid in the battery cells is constantly tested by maintenance men.

WAVEGUIDE PRESSURIZATION ROOM

A waveguide is a rectangular or circular tube made of brass or copper through·which microwave signals can be transmitted. In the Tower, microwave signals travel through waveguides to and from the aerials.

As with the cables, air is pumped into the waveguides at high pressure to avoid the danger of water leaking into the tubes.

AERIALS

The horn and dish aerials, so called because of their shape, are mounted on the outer edges of four circular galleries. They act as mirrors, transmitting and receiving highly concentrated and accurately directed radio beams. These beams carry tens of thousands of simultaneous telephone conversations, television programmes, and signals via the Goonhilly satellite link.

RESTAURANT

The Tower restaurant, above the observation platforms, revolves two and a half times in an hour. (diagram p. 13)

LIFTS

The Tower has two lifts, with a speed of 1,000 feet a minute, which carry passengers to the top of the Tower in 34 seconds.

RADAR

The storm warning radar equipment on the very top of the Tower transmits information direct to Meteorological Office in High Holborn, London.

Hoisting the radar aerial to the top of the lattice mast at the summit of the Post Office Tower called for a great deal of skill and precision

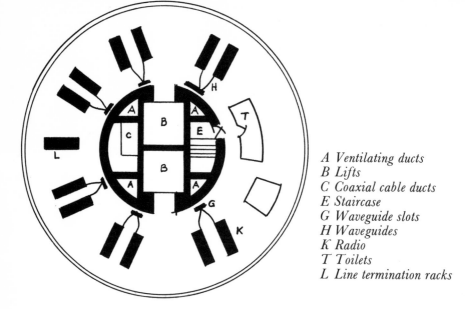

A Ventilating ducts
B Lifts
C Coaxial cable ducts
E Staircase
G Waveguide slots
H Waveguides
K Radio
T Toilets
L Line termination racks

A typical layout of an apparatus floor in the Post Office Tower

MAINTENANCE

A large building like the Post Office Tower provides a great deal of work for its team of maintenance men.

Altogether, the Tower has 50,000 square feet of glass. The windows of both the apparatus rooms and the observation platforms are of special anti-sun glass, $\frac{3}{8}$in. thick, which cuts down the ultra-violet light and prevents over-heating. The heat from the sun is further reduced by the use of double-glazing and aluminium ventilators and sunbreakers, together with the air-conditioning system situated in the central shaft and lower floors of the tower.

In the widest sense, window cleaning is a tall order at the Post Office Tower and three systems are employed. The first is a power-operated carriage, travelling on rails let into the face of the building, that moves up and down and around the apparatus floors. The second system employs cleaning

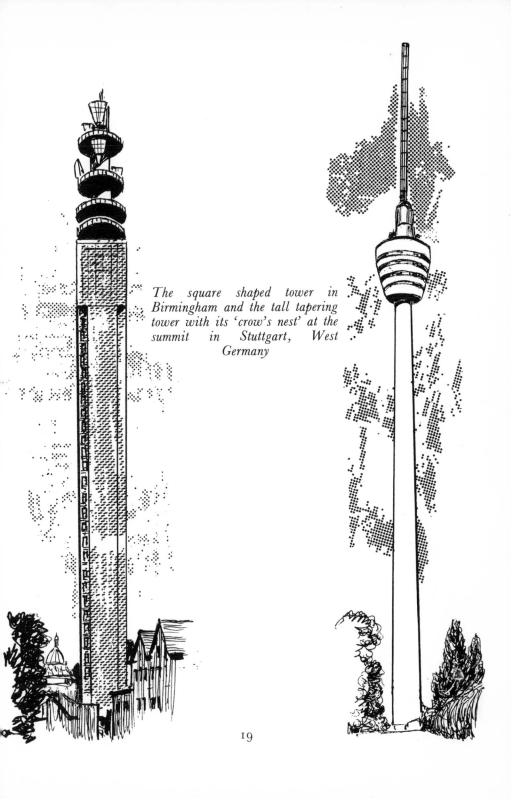

The square shaped tower in Birmingham and the tall tapering tower with its 'crow's nest' at the summit in Stuttgart, West Germany

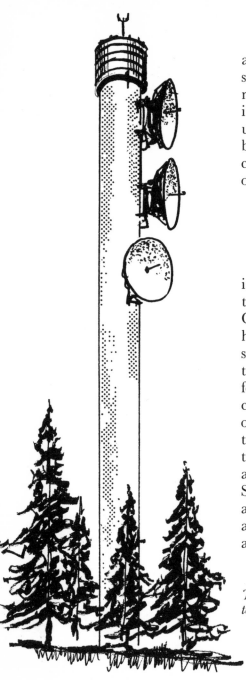

apparatus that remains stationary, while the restaurant revolves against it, and the third system uses a cradle suspended below the restaurant to clean the windows of the observation floors.

WORLD-WIDE DEVELOPMENT OF MICROWAVES

Microwave development is symbolised in Britain by the establishment of the Post Office Tower, the Birmingham Tower, and the many smaller microwave radio towers that will eventually form a chain throughout the country to carry thousands of telephone circuits, and television channels. Some of these smaller towers have already been erected, at Stokenchurch, Charwelton and Cannock Chase, to name a few. There is a tremendous advantage to be gained in

The Swedish microwave tower at Ostersund

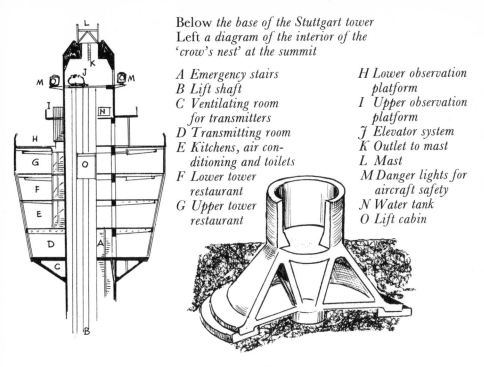

Below *the base of the Stuttgart tower*
Left *a diagram of the interior of the*
'crow's nest' at the summit

A *Emergency stairs*
B *Lift shaft*
C *Ventilating room*
  for transmitters
D *Transmitting room*
E *Kitchens, air con-*
  ditioning and toilets
F *Lower tower*
  restaurant
G *Upper tower*
  restaurant

H *Lower observation*
  platform
I *Upper observation*
  platform
J *Elevator system*
K *Outlet to mast*
L *Mast*
M *Danger lights for*
  aircraft safety
N *Water tank*
O *Lift cabin*

the field of telecommunications by the use of these tall towers to transmit the tens of thousands of trunk calls.

Instead of digging up hundreds, or even thousands of miles of ground to lay cables, the messages are flashed from tower to tower. In the case of a country like Canada, for instance, the tremendous saving of millions of man-hours employed in deep cable laying can easily be imagined. Canada has a network of microwave towers stretching from coast to coast.

The system is invaluable, too, when employed in the so-called underdeveloped countries, because an efficient network of telecommunications can be organised much faster and cheaper, and without digging up the whole country. It must be remembered that due to the earth's curvature, the towers cannot be more than about 30 miles apart, but this is no obstacle, and the system is an ideal one. Our own microwave towers are also used from point to point, of course, but they cannot be employed to transmit across

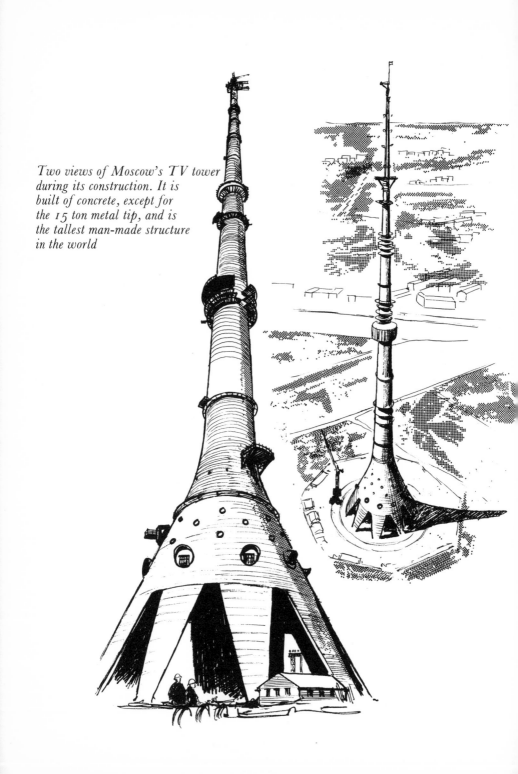

Two views of Moscow's TV tower during its construction. It is built of concrete, except for the 15 ton metal tip, and is the tallest man-made structure in the world

the Atlantic; a tower linking our islands with the United States, and set in the middle of the Atlantic would need to be 400 miles in height. So, by itself, the microwave system offers no solution in this case. The answer, as we have quoted elsewhere, lies in the employment of satellites.

Microwaves are a development of radio transmission, using the higher frequencies of microwaves to get the wider bandwidth for trunkwork. At the moment, the frequencies used in Britain are 2,000, 4,000, and 6,000 M/Hz—the next step will be 11,000 M/Hz, thus giving an even greater number of communication channels.

Britain is in the forefront of modern telecommunications, and has made great contributions in their research and development. She is a member of the 'satellite club', together with the USA, Australia, Canada, Ireland, Japan and most countries of Europe, and the British Post Office has signed up to invest £6 million pounds in the venture.

TELECOMMUNICATIONS

We have seen how the Post Office Tower in London was designed to improve Britain's telecommunication service using the most up-to-date methods available but what, exactly, do we mean by the word telecommunications?

In its widest sense, communication means the connexion between two or more places, the prefix, *tele-*, originating from a Greek word meaning 'far'. The connexions may be by road, rail, or any other form of transport, enabling people to carry information from one place to another in person. Alternatively, the information may be sent by means of signals. Beacons, smoke signals, drums, bells, reflected light, flags and semaphore are all forms of telecommunication which are obviously unsuitable for accurate transmission over long distances. Although still in limited use, they have become less important than telegraph, radio, television using overhead wires, underground cables and microwaves.

The first great step in the history of modern telecommunications was made in 1840 when Wheatstone invented the first really reliable telegraph. It was an apparatus for transmitting signals along cables by means of electrical impulses, and which led to the laying of the first Atlantic cable in 1858.

It was not until 1904 that the actual word 'telecommunications' was first used. It was coined by a Frenchman, M. Estaunié, in his *Traité pratique de télécommunication électrique* where he apologised for adding to an already rich vocabulary this new word that has become so much a part of our daily lives.

CABLES

Cables still play a large and important part in modern telecommunications and especially in telephony. The GPO employs special teams of installation and maintenance men, whose work is now helped enormously by the introduction of modern machinery and equipment.

OVERHEAD CABLES

Telegraph poles bearing overhead cables are a common sight throughout our countryside. In the past, when old poles had to be dug out and new ones erected, the men had hours of hard work with pick and spade. Soon nearly all this work will be carried out with the aid of pole-erecting machines. Instead of employing the labour and time of a team of men, the Pole Erection Units are manned by a two-man crew. Their vehicle carries a load of nine new poles, and is fitted with an ingenious machine which can pull out a pole like an old tooth (exerting a lift of 20 tons), lower a huge auger, drill a deep hole in a few moments, seize a new pole, and drop it into the prepared hole.

Pole and wires often run close to and among branches of trees; this calls for a great deal of branch pruning. This used to be done in the traditional way, with ladders, saws and hooks. Now, electrically-driven tools are used from a hydraulic elevating platform, mounted on a Land Rover. With the ever-increasing demand for telephone services, the new tools and methods are helping to cut costs and manpower time and at the same time the GPO keep a careful watch on all their workers from the safety angle. New machines and time-saving methods count for nothing if men are careless or over-confident.

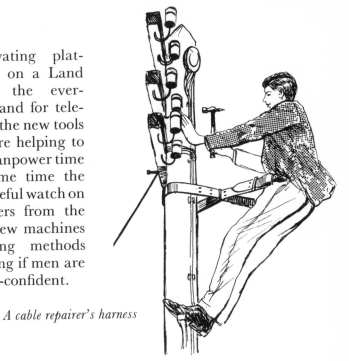

A cable repairer's harness

Mechanical pole erection units uproot old poles, bore holes and lift new poles into position. They can carry nine poles at a time. Here the auger is lowered ready for drilling

Transceiver →

Although most cables now have a protective outer sheath of poly-thene and not lead, the eight-foot diameter drums are still very heavy and have to be lifted on jacks. Here a cable gang feed the cable into a duct section while listening to instructions given over a transceiver or walkie-talkie set (below)

UNDERGROUND CABLES

More and more cables today are being laid underground. All cables, whether for telephone, telegraph or television, have a protective sheath around them to insulate them and protect them from the damp, and poly-thene is steadily replacing lead as the most suitable material for it. It is cheaper, cleaner and lighter and can

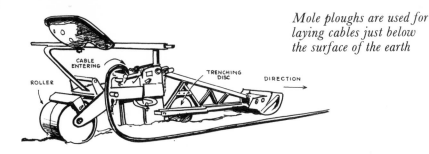

Mole ploughs are used for laying cables just below the surface of the earth

ROLLER
CABLE ENTERING
TRENCHING DISC
DIRECTION

be used in much longer lengths. This long-length cabling has led to the use of portable radio sets by the installation crews. A technician can use the walkie-talkie set to talk to his colleagues and report the arrival of a cable at a joining point several hundred yards away.

Before new cable can be laid, roads have to be opened and ducting installed, for cables need more substantial protection from damage than their outer sheaths can give them. Ducts are tubes or pipes which are both airtight and watertight and inside which the cables are laid. Ducts made of earthenware are still being used, and give excellent service. They are cheap to instal, and in addition, their glazed surface enables cable to be pulled through without damaging the outer sheathing. On the other hand, the GPO say they are heavy to transport, easily damaged in transit, and require a high standard of jointing to make them watertight. Other materials are being tested by GPO engineers, notably PVC.

Telephone cables contain over one hundred separate wires which must be carefully joined together and then sealed with lead

PRESSURIZATION OF UNDERGROUND CABLES

You may recall the pressure gauges in the Cable Chamber back at the Tower. Today, most of the underground cables in the Post Office network are being pressurised with dry air, the air inside the sheaths being kept at about 9 lbs a square inch. The greatest enemy of the underground cable engineer is the entry of water into the cables once the sheaths have become damaged. Cables are subject to several hazards, such as corrosion, cracking of sheaths due to vibration, track subsidence, or direct damage made by other service workers on roadworks for gas, water, electricity, or sewerage repair work, and sometimes by gas explosions or burst water mains. Due to the pressurising system, an air leak can be located quite accurately, and a repair can be carried out at the spot without having to replace a complete cable length.

The air that is introduced under pressure to the cable network has to be carefully prepared first. It is filtered to remove dust particles and then compressed and cooled to remove all traces of moisture. To safeguard against an accidental delivery of damp air caused by a fault in the drying equipment, a moisture-detecting unit is placed in the air line. This instrument stops the compressor and sounds an alarm if there is a dangerous rise in water-content. In the Post Office Tower the air-pressurising equipment and alarm units are situated in the basement.

REPEATERS

One of the biggest obstacles to the development of long-long-distance telephony was the fact that electric currents decrease in strength as the length of wire increases. This has now been overcome by the use of 'repeaters', which are introduced at certain points on long distance routes, and which increase or amplify the current received, sending it on to the next repeater where it is again amplified. By these means, it reaches its destination with no loss, and just as

Transistors are assembled inside a dust-free humidity cabinet by highly trained operators. They are a vital part of repeaters necessary to amplify signals on overhead, underground and under sea cables

though the distance was a short one. This amplification is achieved by valves, and more recently by transistors. It is only by the use of these repeaters that we are able to speak over great distances, not only in Great Britain, but also across the sea to every country linked with us by submarine cable or radio-telephone.

SUBMARINE CABLES

The work of the men who laid the first telephone cables on the sea beds makes a stirring tale of hardship and danger, but even today, with large up-to-date ships with all modern aids, the job is not easy. The first telephone cable, with two circuits, was laid across the English Channel in 1850 by the men of the tug *Goliath*. Since then, the ocean beds of the world have become the home of thousands of miles of submarine cable, the vital links that enable the human voice to be carried around the world. But even as recently as eleven

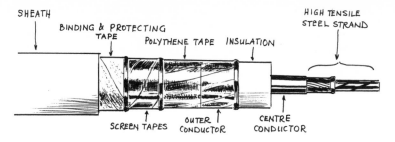

SHEATH

BINDING & PROTECTING
TAPE

POLYTHENE TAPE   INSULATION

HIGH TENSILE
STEEL STRAND

SCREEN TAPES   OUTER
CONDUCTOR

CENTRE
CONDUCTOR

The new light-weight under-sea cables are little more than an inch in diameter and have a central core of 43 high grade steel strands which can withstand a pull of more than seven tons. An insulation of polythene separates a copper tube and aluminium tapes which carry the electrical signals

years ago, transatlantic cables were used simply to transmit messages by electrical impulses. Morse code played a large part in this kind of telegraphy.

The big change came for undersea cable communications with the development of the 'repeaters' or amplifiers to boost the signals at intervals along the cable lengths. Power to operate these is fed at high voltage over the cable itself.

Highly skilled technicans work in conditions very like those in an operating theatre when assembling the complex deep-water repeaters

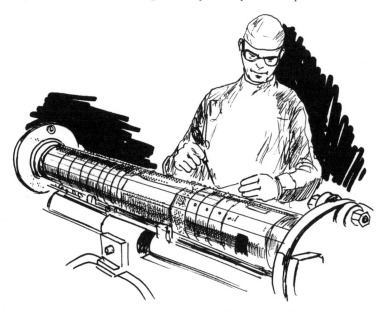

The repeaters are laid at intervals of about 30 miles along the cable, and have two amplifiers working in parallel, so that if one fails, the other maintains service. These repeaters cost about £18,000 each. The first operational repeater was laid in 1946, and after that it took ten hard years of research and planning before the first transatlantic telephone cable system was laid in 1956 between Scotland and Newfoundland.

Today, there is a total of some 65,000 miles of cable under the oceans, involving thousands of submerged repeaters. It was an outstanding event in communications history when on 2nd December, 1963, the voice of Her Majesty the Queen travelled 16,000 miles from London to Sydney, and was

Maintenance and repair of cables and repeaters is the main part of the work of a cable ship's crew. Here a transistorized repeater is taken aboard HMTS Iris

clearly heard simultaneously in five countries—in Britain, Canada, Fiji, New Zealand and Australia. This was a great step forward in the expansion and improvement of the British Commonwealth Communication links. This cable line is called COMPAC (*Com*munications in *Pac*ific), and is the first to be laid across the Pacific Ocean, joining Canada with Australia and New Zealand by way of Hawaii and Fiji. It forms the second link in the Commonwealth Telephone Cable System and together with CANTAT (*Can*ada *T*ransatlantic *T*elephones) which linked Canada and Scotland in 1961 it enables people on the opposite sides of the earth to speak to each other over circuits which do not suffer from the fading and interference of the high frequency radio links they replace.

Now, if you want to speak from somewhere in Britain to, let us say, a relative in Australia, your voice will go from your home to your local exchange, be routed to a trunk exchange, then to the Post Office Tower in London. From there, it could be switched to Scotland. From then, it dives under the sea by CANTAT cable to Montreal, where it is beamed across Canada to Vancouver by the microwave system. Then on it goes under the sea again by COMPAC to Hawaii, Suva, Auckland and across to Sydney, Australia. Your aunt's voice will be as clear as though she were phoning from across the street!

CABLE SHIPS

The Post Office's fleet of four cable ships has played a major part in providing some of the important undersea cable links throughout the world. They are specially equipped and designed to cope with the job of laying, storing, splicing, and maintaining many of these cables. The ships are HMTS *Monarch, Alert, Iris,* and *Ariel,* the two former being the larger. Their holds can store hundreds of miles of submarine cable, coiled with neatness and precision. The

HMTS Monarch, *one of the GPO's four cable ships*

ships also carry repeaters, buoys, and every kind of equipment for salvaging and repairing broken cables. On board, there are complete engineering workshops, able to cope with modern repair methods and materials.

Quite frequently, submarine telephone cables suffer damage from various causes, sometimes from deep-sea trawlers, whose trawling gear is often lost through entanglement with the cables. Sea and air patrols are mounted, to warn the fishermen of the presence of cables underneath the sea. At the present time, the cables are not marked on navigation charts because of Government restrictions; but in the interests of preserving the cables, these restrictions are being eased. Trawler owners have been known to cut a cable when their trawl has brought one to the surface, which is a punishable offence. Under the terms of the International Convention of 1884 for the protection of submarine cables, any owner of a vessel who could prove that he had sacrificed an anchor, a net, or other fishing gear in order to avoid damaging a cable would be compensated by the owner of

33

the cable. The best thing a skipper can do if his trawl accidentally hooks one up is to sacrifice the gear and claim compensation for it.

If you have seen a cable ship, you may have noticed the cabling guides at bow and stern: such a ship can be identified by these 'whiskers', as they are called. HMTS *Monarch* has recently been fitted with whiskers of a new pattern, because although the advent of the new lightweight cables brought many advantages, they also introduced some problems in cable handling.

To assist in repair and recovery work, the *Monarch* has a new retractable observation platform, equipped with engine-room telegraph, compass repeater, and other navigational aids, which are used by the officer controlling the work. He now has a clearer and better all-round view of the area around and under the whiskers where the cable emerges from the water. This is of the utmost importance at the bows, since it is here that the most complicated operations of grappling and splicing take place.

Cable ships have 'whiskers' at bow and stern, to guide the cables leaving the ship. HMTS Monarch *has 'whiskers' specially designed to avoid damage to the new light-weight cables*

Corner of manual telephone exchange
(see page 37)

TELEPHONES

Let us examine what happens when you lift a telephone receiver to call a friend, and speak into it. When somebody speaks, the vibration of his vocal cords causes tiny changes in the air pressure in his mouth. These pressure changes radiate from the speaker in waves, just as little ripples are caused by lightly touching the surface of a bowl of water. In this case, air is the medium which carries sound waves to another person's ears. If you talk very loudly, the pressure of the waves will be strong and the sound loud, but as the waves radiate out to a distance, they become weaker until at last they cannot be heard. An electric current can be transmitted over wires to quite a large distance without much loss. If speech sound waves can be changed to a similar

A cable pressurization rack in an exchange. There is one gauge for each trunk of junction cable leaving the exchange

rising and falling electric current—to be later converted back again to sound—the distance over which speech can be sent is obviously greatly increased. The modern telephone works on this simple principle.

A telephone consists of a transmitter, which converts sound waves to a varying electric current corresponding to them, and a receiver which changes the current back into sound waves of the original type.

The telephone *transmitter* consists of a metal diaphragm and a box containing granules of carbon which lightly touch the diaphragm's centre. When you speak into the mouthpiece of the transmitter, the diaphragm vibrates; these vibrations cause varying pressure on the granules, through which an electric current is passed. When the sound wave pressure increases, the carbon particles are pushed closer together. The tighter they squeeze together, the easier the current flows. When pressure eases, they become less squeezed and the current flows less freely. So the sound waves causing the diaphragm to vibrate are reproduced in the form of increases and decreases in the flow of the current through the transmitter. This current is sent over a pair of wires to a distant receiver.

The *receiver's* job is to change the fluctuating current back into sound waves. It is different from the transmitter, in that it consists of a metal diaphragm tightly held round its circumference and placed very close to, but not touching, the poles of a strong magnet. A large number of turns of fine wire are wound around the magnet forming a coil. The magnet normally attracts the diaphragm with a constant pull, but when a varying current is sent through the coil, the pull increases (or decreases) with the variation in the current. The fluctuating current from the transmitter is passed through the coil, and rapid, everchanging variations are produced in the strength of the magnet, which attracts the diaphragm in a similar degree, causing it to vibrate in unison with the diaphragm in the transmitter, and thus create sound waves which you hear as a voice.

When Graham Bell invented the telephone, it enabled two people to talk to each other over a distance. Each needed a transmitter and receiver in the circuit. Telephone exchanges did not exist; telephonic contact between a number of people was quite unmanageable—just consider—by direct connection, six people would need 15 lines, while ten thousand would need about 50,000,000!

THE EXCHANGE
a. Manual

Telephone exchanges solved the problem of connecting a large number of subscribers to each other. Exchanges can be operated manually or automatically. In a manual exchange, each connection is made by the telephone operator; in an automatic exchange the machine does this work. In manual exchanges (most offices, hotels, etc. have manual exchanges), the wires from the telephones end at switchboards. Using flexible wires fitted with plugs at their ends (called 'cords'), an operator can connect any two subscribers' circuits together. When you lift your receiver, a switch operates, and a current flows through the circuit and lights a tiny lamp on the exchange switchboard. When the operator inserts one of the cords in your line, she can speak to you, and you can then ask for your number. She then inserts the other end of the cord in the required line and operates a switch to ring your correspondent's bell. When you call is finished, both receivers are replaced, and 'clearing' signal lamps come on at the exchange switchboard. The operator then knows the call is finished and she withdraws the cord, disconnecting the circuit.

b. Automatic

An automatic telephone exchange connects one subscriber's telephone with another, without the aid of an operator. On an automatic exchange, all you do to call a subscriber is to lift the receiver and operate your dial; when you do this, several things happen. Automatic 'selectors' come into action, controlled by the numbers you have dialled, and the connection between you and the number you want is completed as soon as the last figure is dialled.

The dial, when returning to its normal position, creates electrical impulses corresponding to the number dialled, and which travel along the circuit and operate the selectors. (If you keep your ear to the transmitter when dialling, you can hear the tiny clicking noises corresponding to the electrical impulses.) The selector has a hundred contacts, arranged in rows of ten. A switch-arm (or wiper) moves up in steps to the row determined by the 'thousands' figure dialled (in the case of a four-digit number), then passes round the row of contacts, stopping at the first disengaged one. This contact gives access to the next selector which, by repeating the process, accepts the 'hundreds' digit as it is dialled, and then extends the connection to the final selector. On receiving the impulses corresponding to the 'tens' digit, the switch-arm of this selector moves up to the appropriate row but does not pass along the row until the 'units' figure is dialled. When this is done, the arm moves along the row to the contact determined by the last figure dialled, thus completing the connection to the dialled subscriber's line. The switching process is now complete and the called telephone rings automatically.

In many cities, telephone numbers include letters as well as figures, and subscribers' numbers are shown with the first three letters in capitals—e.g.—MAYfair 1234. Dialling the letters or the numerical code which precedes the number produces impulses on an additional piece of apparatus known as the director, which automatically selects a free line to the wanted exchange. It then passes on the impulses of the numbers as they are dialled, to operate the selectors at the distant exchange.

There are special code numbers for obtaining the operator, and in practically all automatic areas 999 is dialled in emergency to obtain an operator who will connect to the required service—Police, Fire Brigade, Ambulance or, in coastal areas, Coastguard.

DIALLING TONES

Special pieces of equipment, which at first sight look like little dynamos, give out the appropriate dialling tones:
a—a constant purring when you lift the receiver to dial.
b—the called number being rung (the ringing tone—burr-burr).

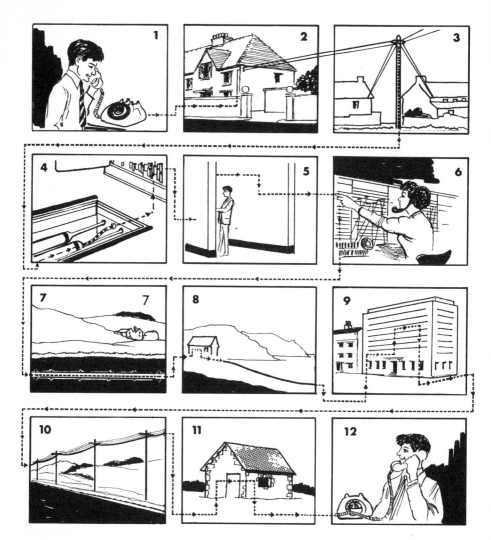

This diagram shows the route of an imaginary trunk call. The caller dials (1) and his voice, changed into electronic impulses, leaves the house (2), travels over the wires to a distribution pole (3), along a cable to a distribution box (4) and to the exchange (5). The operator connects the call (6), and the signals continues along an underground cable (7) to an undersea cable (8), and on to a distant exchange (9). They then pass along an overhead pole route (10) to a small unattended automatic exchange ((1)) and finally into the receiver of the caller's friend

c—engaged sound—a repeated single high-pitched note.

d—unobtainable sound—a steady high-pitched note.

e—a new tone (paytone) may be heard during calls from Subscriber Trunk Dialling areas. 'Paytone' (rapid pips) is heard only from a 'pay-on-answer' coinbox and indicates to the caller that his number has been connected and that he should now insert his money.

SUBSCRIBER TRUNK DIALLING—STD

In some areas you can now dial your own trunk calls, because of recent developments in automatic telephony. New apparatus, called Group Routing and Charging Equipment (GRACE for short) has been designed, which connects these calls and at the same time registers the charge on your meter. The GPO hope to extend GRACE to cover more than 90 per cent of the United Kingdom by 1970. The task of this ingenious new equipment is to interpret the signals made by you when you dial, steer the call through the network of trunk lines to its destination, and when the call is answered, to control the recording of the charge on your meter. When you wish to call someone by STD, you dial a simple code before dialling his number: the code always starts with '0', which connects you to GRACE.

THE SPEAKING CLOCK SERVICE—TIM

Is provided by the British Post Office, and can be obtained by dialling the digits '123' or the letters TIM. The clock has a memory in the form of a drum or sleeve (very much like a tape recorder). The various phrases such as 'at the third stroke it will be "one", "two", "three" etc., and "one", "two", or "three seconds"' are recorded on the drum surface and assembled into the announcements to cover the 24-hour period by switching devices. There are two such clock installations, one in London and the other in Liverpool; these cover the whole country. Each installation comprises a 'main' and standby machine, and the time is checked daily by comparison with the Time Standard from the Royal Observatory at Hurstmonceaux. The clocks are accurate to within one twentieth of a second. The digits '123' are used to indicate to the local exchange that the correct time is required by the caller, and this results in a connection to the nearest distribution point for the announcement.

Britain is changing over from exchange names to all-figure telephone numbers. This will make it much easier for people abroad to make trunk calls to Britain. These are all-figure dials from Egypt, Russia and Hong Kong, taken from a GPO journal

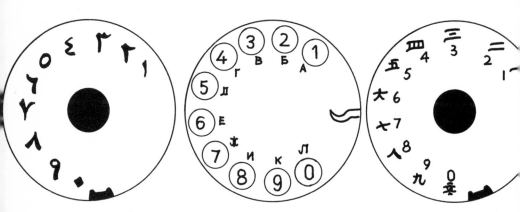

ALL FIGURES BY 1970

For nearly 40 years telephone numbers in Britain's big cities have been a mixture of letters and numbers. This system was first adopted in London when automatic telephones were introduced and it extended in time to other large cities. Now, the letter-figure combinations have almost disappeared. The GPO hope that very soon all telephones in Britain will have all-figure numbers. This conversion, costing over a million pounds, is expected to speed and expand the telephone services both here and overseas.

Although some people would prefer to keep exchange names, considering them easier to remember, the GPO see many advantages in the change to numbers. It will help the expansion of the inland telephone service and, most important of all, it will help the dialling of international calls.

Britain is now one of the very few countries which has letters and figures in its telephone numbers, and this handicaps people in other countries who want to dial their calls to British subscribers. The USA, Canada and France are now changing to all-figure dialling, and unless we follow, say the GPO, we'll soon be the only country in Western Europe to have mixed letter and figure numbers. If we wish to keep our place as one of the world's leading business and trading centres, the sooner we change over to all-figures, the better.

It is expected that by the end of the century, there will be 600 million telephones throughout the world, Great Britain having a share in the region of 20 million. Most of them will be able to dial direct to anywhere in the world.

TELEGRAMS

Let us take a brief look at the telegram service and how it works, at the Central Telegraph Office in London. On an average day 6,000 telegrams are dealt with at the CTO, which is responsible for the delivery of incoming telegrams to the EC1 and EC4 districts during the day, and the whole of the London area at night. Every outgoing telegram from the whole of the London area to the United Kingdom and Eire is dealt with in the Main Telegraph Room. They are received by telephone from three sources—the ordinary public, telephone call-boxes, and smaller Post Offices which pass on telegrams handed in across the counter. There is a system by which any calls to 'Telegrams' are routed in the order in which they are made, to disengaged operators. Any call that does not get immediate attention is held in a 'queue' until it can be dealt with, but because as many as fifty operators are available at one time in taking down telegrams, delays of more than a few seconds are rare.

The message is typed out on a tape using a phonogram machine, a special kind of typewriter which produces only capital letters. As the scores of operators sit at their machines facing each other, a central conveyor between them whisks the message away for outward transmission by the tele-printer operator. Nowadays, if you are on the phone, tele-grams are read to you from the nearest Post Office, but many telegrams still have to be delivered by the boys on red motor-cycles. On special occasions, people like to send the attractive Greetings Telegrams, and these, to obtain the best effect, must be delivered by hand.

TELEX—TALKING BY TYPEWRITER

Fleet Building in Farringdon Street, London has fifteen storeys, and contains some of the most up-to-date telecom equipment in the world; it is also the home of the Telex service. What is Telex? It really means typewriting over wires. Telex involves the use of a machine looking like a large typewriter, which reproduces the message and at the

If the person who is to receive a telegram is on the telephone, it is usually read out to him over the phone. Otherwise, it is delivered to him by hand at top speed by a 'telegram boy' on a red GPO motorcycle

A Teleprinter

same time causes another teleprinter at the other end of a pair of wires to type the same message simultaneously. How does it work? As with the telephone, you first dial the number required; when connected, you don't talk but type your message. It is changed into electronic impulses which travel along cables in much the same way as your voice when you speak into a telephone. Other people with teleprinters can dial your number and send messages to you. A large organisation like the London Fire Brigade can send a message to dozens of local Fire Stations instantaneously by the Telex service. Large firms can transmit or receive typed messages (switched through the International Telex Exchange) from many parts of the world. It is far superior to either a letter or a phone call in giving or receiving complicated information, or in placing or receiving orders. Letters travel but slowly, while telephone messages can be misunderstood, but the message from a teleprinter is immediate and clear. Using a teleprinter is very simple. You find the number you want, and press the 'dial' button on the dialling unit. A green bulb lights and shows that the circuit is ready. Then you dial the wanted number and are connected immediately. At this, the distant teleprinter sends automatically its 'answer-back' code, and you check that you have the right number. You send your own 'answerback' to let them know who you are—then you simply type your message. When you have finished, you send your answerback code and get the distant machine's code by operating the 'D' key.

For incoming calls, the green lamp lights up and the teleprinter motor starts. Your answer-back code is automatically sent to the caller, you receive their code, and the message follows. Provided the power is left switched on, calls can be received at any time of the day or night. This is useful for business people, who get calls from other parts of the world, and where time varies from British Standard Time.

DATEL—DATA BY TELEPHONE

Datel caters for subscribers who want to send small quantities of data, perhaps daily, from a number of points to a central office. This service ensures against inaccuracies which always occur when data is relayed by voice over a telephone. It is a boon for companies owning say, a chain of shoe or grocery shops, since it provides a new, quick method of stocktaking. In a shoe shop, this is achieved by inserting a punched tabulator card containing details of shoe size, colour, and name of manufacturer in each shoe box, and retaining the card after the shoes are sold. These details can then be transmitted by Datel Service to the head office, where a day-to-day indication of stock position and sales trends can be kept. To equip a group of shops with the Datel service, each branch needs a Datel Modem No 3 or No 5. (A Modem is a piece of equipment measuring about 16 ins. by 20 ins. by 4 ins., with rows of buttons and switches, and is connected to the shop's telephone circuit.)

All these Modems are connected to the head office of the firm, which have Modems No 4 or No 6 installed and which, in turn, are linked to a data processor. These Modems translate the data into telephone line signals at the transmitting end, and reverse the process at the receiving end. Operating procedure merely involves an operator at a branch shop phoning head office and, after a word with her opposite number, both switch to the Datel Modems. The information is then transmitted.

RADIO

Radio does not play as large a part in telecommunications as one might imagine. The low frequency signals which follow the curve of the earth are easily disturbed by bad weather conditions and are not suitable for long-distance communications. Over shorter distances, however, radio can supply a very important communications link for shipping, although perfect voice transmission is not possible.

'SHIP TO SHORE' SERVICE

Around our coasts are the twelve remote and isolated Post Office coast radio stations with the romantic names of Oban, Portpatrick, Anglesey, Portishead, Ilfracombe, Land's End, Niton, North Foreland, Humber, Cullercoats, Stonehaven and Wick. Ship to shore communication by radio is of the utmost value to shipping. Through the radiotelegraph and radiotelephone services at the coast stations, ship owners are able to direct their vessels at sea. The stations contribute to safety at sea by broadcasting weather forecasts, navigational and gale warnings, and by giving direct assistance to ships in trouble through their Distress and Safety of Life at Sea services. All these radio stations except Portishead, which watches over ships outside the range of the other eleven, keep a continuous watch on the International Distress frequencies for calls for help. Immediately the signal 'SOS' (MAYDAY on radiotelephony) comes through, all attention is directed on the ship in trouble. As soon as the distress message is received, the station uses a special radio signal to ring automatic alarm bells on ships in the area to alert the Radio Officers. The station then broadcasts details of the casualty to all ships in the area, and at the same time sends information by telephone or teleprinter to Rescue Authorities; in particular to the Coast-

Coastal Radio Station

guard, the Naval Authorities and Lloyds of London. If
the coastguards become involved, they co-ordinate rescue
operations, calling out lifeboats or life-saving parties with
their apparatus for cliff rescue, or with the help of the RAF,
search aircraft, air-sea rescue helicopters and high-speed
launches. If a sinking ship has had to be abandoned, the
passengers and crew may be adrift in lifeboats or rafts. They
must be found, taken to safety, and doctors and ambulances
alerted to receive them. In this vital work, the Coast Station
is the focal point of communication, controlling and maintaining contact between those at sea and on shore. This
marine service of the Post Office was born in 1909, when the
Lizard Radio Station was purchased from the Marconi
International Marine Communication Company, together
with five other stations at Niton, Caister, Seaforth, Rosslare
and Crookhaven. Two more were acquired from Lloyds,
Malin Head and North Foreland. These eight stations with
a staff of forty, provided a short-range distress and R/T
service for the 286 British ships equipped with radio, as
well as radio-equipped foreign ships. Back in 1910, that
tiny staff dealt with nearly 50,000 messages. Today, the
Post Office staff of 225 handle 86,000 messages each year,
and act as shore links for 6,300 British and 3,000 foreign ships.

*Mobile Ground Station
in Western Germany*

SATELLITES

We have seen how telephone, television, and radio links can be carried from one continent to another by means of under-sea cables and repeaters. Until recently this was the only satisfactory method of inter-continental communications.

The introduction of the microwave links, which work on a very high frequency and are not, therefore, subject to the same interference as long wave radio links, has revolutionized the field of telecommunications. We have seen how towers, like our own in London, are springing up to provide efficient networks.

Since, however, microwave signals travel in a straight line, and since the surface of the earth is curved, it would be impossible to build a tower high enough to transmit signals across the Atlantic. The Moscow tower, a third of a mile high, can only relay to a distance of 75 miles.

Man's discovery that he could send an artificial satellite into orbit around the earth solved the problem. A microwave repeater placed in a satellite thousands of miles above the earth could span whole continents and oceans. When the National Aeronautics and Space Administration of the United States (NASA) began to develop this new tech-

It has recently been discovered that satellites in orbit can be used for amplifying and redirecting microwave beams. Here a satellite-bearing rocket leaves the launching pad

nology in 1958, a form of earth-space communications had already been tried. In 1946, the US Army Signal Corps had made radar contact with the moon, and conversation was possible between Washington and Hawaii by reflecting signals off the moon's surface. The moon was used as a communication satellite, but it proved impractical for regular transmissions. There are two kinds of satellite—passive and active. The moon had acted as the former, behaving as a radio mirror reflecting signals transmitted to it. The active type of satellite amplifies and re-transmits the signals it receives. Of the two, the passive is simpler and more reliable, for it has no working parts. However, it requires very powerful transmitters and sensitive receivers on the ground.

'ECHO'

NASA's first experimental satellite, Echo 1 was a passive one. It was launched into orbit in August 1960. An aluminium-coated nylar polyester balloon with a skin 500-millionths of an inch thick, Echo 1 left the earth folded inside a canister 26 inches in diameter, and was launched by a Delta rocket. Once in its 1,000 mile orbit, Echo 1 was ejected from its container and a special substance inside it changed from solid state to gas, expanding the balloon to 100 feet in diameter. Its weight was 124 lbs. Echo 1 proved once and for all that it was possible to use man-made passive satellites. The signals reflected from it made possible long-distance telephone conversations, and the transmission of photographs and music.

Echo 2 followed in 1964, placed in orbit by a Thor-Agena rocket; it has remained unchanged since its first day in orbit, and is circling the earth once every 109 minutes. Like Echo 1 it is a passive satellite.

'SCORE'

Active satellites, which amplify signals received from one ground station and re-transmit them to another, are far more complicated than the mirror type, but this is somewhat offset by the fact that much simpler apparatus is needed at the ground stations. In 1958, an Atlas rocket launched a relay satellite called SCORE into orbit. It carried a radio transmitter, and in its short life of 30 days, demonstrated its ability to relay voice, code, and teletype messages.

The first Telstar satellite was launched in July 1963. Sapphire blue and silver in colour, it measured 34 inches across and was made up of 15,000 separate parts

'TELSTAR'

The famous project Telstar was developed by the American Telephone and Telegraph Company together with NASA, and the first of the two satellites, Telstar 1, was launched in July 1963 by a three-stage Delta rocket. Satellite Telstar received a great deal of public attention, and some 50 television programmes were exchanged between US and European television stations, in black and white and in colour. Telephone calls were made in both directions, and telephotos were relayed by it. Due to Telstar's contribution to international communications, ground stations were established in Italy, Brazil, Germany, Japan, Sweden and Spain by late 1964. For four months Telstar 1 worked as planned, but in February 1963, after failing to respond to commands from the ground, it went silent.

Telstar 2 followed Telstar 1, but the farthest point it reached from the earth in its orbit is almost doubled. The higher altitude keeps it out of the high radiation regions of space for the greater part of the 225 minute orbiting time, and also provides it with longer periods when it is visible from, and can communicate with, European and US ground stations. It, too, went silent for nearly a month but with that exception it is functioning well.

'RELAY'

The little Nasa Relay 1 was launched in December 1962, and was used in communication experiments between the US and Europe, South America and Japan. It is only 33 inches long, and weighs 172 lbs. Its mast-like antenna is used to receive and transmit a single television broadcast or twelve simultaneous two-way telephone conversations. More than 8,000 solar cells mounted in its eight sides charge the batteries which power it. It had a design life of a year, but it continued to operate well for another 13 months. Relay 2 is an improved model, with greater reliability and a resistance to radiation damage. It was sent up in January 1964, into a slightly higher orbit than Relay 1, made possible

The Relay satellite is 33 inches long, and weighs 172 lbs. A mast-like antenna extending an additional 18 inches at one end is used to receive and transmit a single television broadcast or twelve simultaneous two-way telephone conversations. Four whip antennae at the other end of the prism handle control and tracking and relay information on the satellite's performance

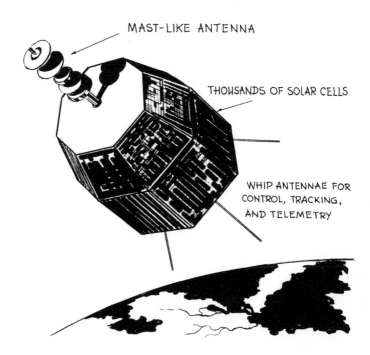

MAST-LIKE ANTENNA

THOUSANDS OF SOLAR CELLS

WHIP ANTENNAE FOR
CONTROL, TRACKING,
AND TELEMETRY

by the improved perform-
ance of the Delta launch
rocket's second stage. It has
been used for many trans-
atlantic and transpacific television news transmissions,
among these being the
coverage of the 1964 Winter
Olympics from Europe, the
first TV transmissions from
Japan, and the opening of
the World's Fair in New
York.

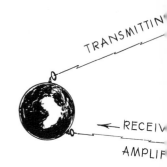

'SYNCOM'

The Project SYNCOM was Nasa's next undertaking; the
purpose was to place repeater satellites in a synchronous
orbit, that is, an orbit in which the satellite would make its
revolution round the earth in the same period of time (24
hours) that it takes the earth to make a complete revolution

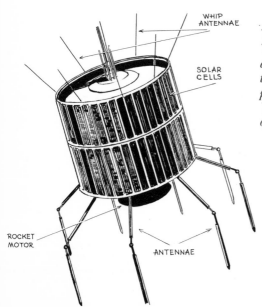

*This is one of the three types of Applications
Technology (APT) Satellites. The eight whip
antennae control the movement and working of
the satellite, and those at the base relay telephone conversations and television programmes.
The satellite runs on power from the thousands
of solar cells on its surface*

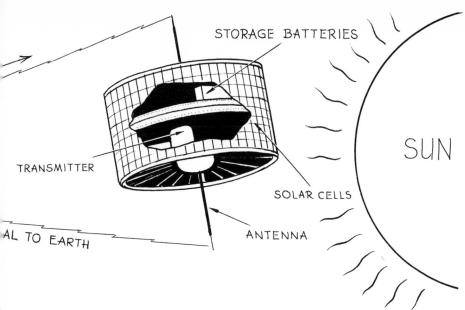

STORAGE BATTERIES

SUN

TRANSMITTER

SOLAR CELLS

AL TO EARTH

ANTENNA

Transmitting and receiving stations are often too far apart round the earth's curve to be able to transmit to each other direct. Instead, they transmit signals to a satellite which, working on power from its solar cells, amplifies them and transmits them back to the receiving station on earth. We receive 'live' television programmes from America this way

on its axis. The altitude the satellite would have to reach to achieve this orbit was worked out to be 22,237 miles; from such a height, a vast amount of the earth's surface could be covered. One synchronous satellite would be able to provide uninterrupted communication service twenty-four hours a day. Moreover, if the satellite's orbit was circular as well (rather than elliptical) and lying in the plane of the earth's equator, it would appear from earth to be stationary. Three such satellites, properly positioned, could serve almost the entire world. Syncom 1 was not a complete success, but Syncom 2 reached the orbit intended for it, except for one thing—it had not achieved *equatorial* orbit. Instead of appearing to hang over one spot on the earth, it traced a slender figure 8 in the sky as it moved north and south of the equator. With Syncom 3, this error was reduced to a fraction, and thus it really appeared to be stationary— hanging like a tiny star in the sky.

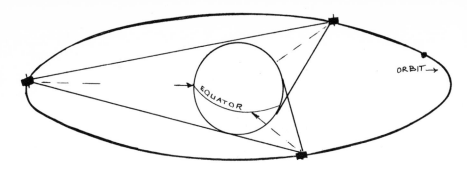

Repeater satellites in synchronous orbit would encircle the earth in the same time (24 hours) that it takes the earth to revolve on its axis, which means that from the earth they would appear 'fixed' in the sky. The diagram shows how three of them could cover most of the earth's surface

Nasa's future project is called the Applications Technology Satellite (ATS); they are planning a five-flight programme throughout 1969. Many new experiments are envisaged in the field of meteorology, navigation, radiation detection and radio propagation. Satellites have brought the big breakthrough to the science of telecommunications; they can be the means of bringing educational and instructional material to the most remote places on earth.

TRACKING STATIONS

Britain has its own satellite tracking station at Goonhilly, on a stretch of moorland in Cornwall. It was built in 1961, and in the next year came the historic transatlantic transmissions by way of Telstar. There are many such earth stations in several countries, but they all have one thing in common—a huge dish-shaped aerial. Recently, Goonhilly's dish aerial has been modified and made shallower than the previous one. The original dish aerial had been quite satisfactory in handling the signals from the earlier satellites, but the recent ones are five or six times more distant. A very much higher degree of accuracy and precision was called for in the construction of the aerial.

The parabolic dish type of aerial used at Goonhilly can be likened to the mirror reflector of a searchlight or a car headlight, in which the source of light at the focus is converted into a narrow beam of light after reflection from the

At Goonhilly, only five
miles from where Marconi
sent the first radio signal
to America, the Post Office
Satellite Ground Station
turns its huge dish aerial
to the sky. It not only
transmits signals but also
amplifies and records signals
received from satellites

The aerial steering room in the control tower at Goonhilly.
The engineer corrects faults indicated by the instruments on
the console and can steer the giant aerial

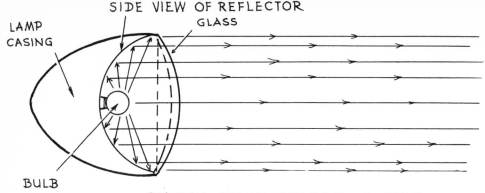

SIDE VIEW OF REFLECTOR

GLASS

LAMP CASING

BULB

DIAGRAM SHOWS BEAMS FROM BULB STRIKING REFLECTOR AND BEING CONVERTED INTO A STRAIGHT BEAM OF LIGHT

The Goonhilly dish aerial sends out concentrated beams of signals rather like light from a car's headlamp. The curved mirror of the reflector concentrates light from the bulb into one straight beam. Without the reflector, the bulb would give out a very feeble light, for rays would be lost in all directions

mirror. In an aerial, there is no lamp at the focus but a source of radio energy (known as the feed) and the system works two ways; besides producing a narrow beam of transmitted power, radio signals from a distant point arriving at the reflector are concentrated on to the focus where they can be led to the maser receiver.

A 'maser' (the word is an abbreviation of Microwave Amplification by the Stimulated Emmission of Radiation) is an amplifier of microwave frequencies. A maser amplifier forms the first receiving stage at Goonhilly, and is used to amplify the signal which is received from the satellite at a power level of about a millionth part of a millionth part of a watt.

Countries making use of the satellites may not do so free of charge. On 20th August 1964, the United Kingdom signed an agreement in Washington which makes us a partner in arrangements for the establishment of the 'Space Sector'. This would be one single satellite system round the globe which would be used for commercial communications. Besides the USA, other partners consist of Australia, Canada, Eire, Japan, and most countries of Europe. The

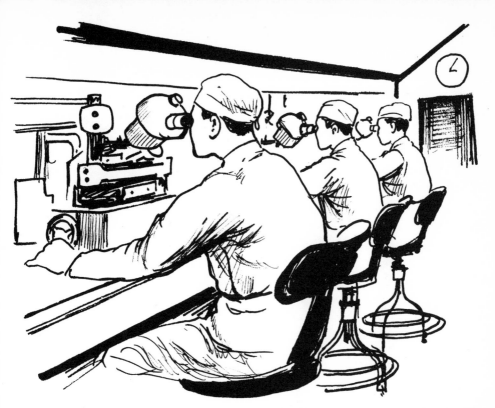

Transistor assembly at Dollis Hill

agreement commits the GPO to invest six million pounds spread over five years in the venture, and the Post Office secures a seat on the International Committee.

INTO THE FUTURE

Great advances are still being made in the field of tele-communications and the Post Office has its own Engineering Research Station at Dollis Hill in North-west London. There scientists and technologists are experimenting with various means of expanding telecommunications and improving the message-carrying capacity of the microwave links which are being set up all over the country.

Experiments are also being made to improve telephone equipment. Dollis Hill has produced new designs for push-button telephones; television cameras are being used to study the way the handset is held in relation to the user's

The Deltaline interphone (right), *and the Trimphone* (left),
two of the GPO's latest telephone designs

mouth when new telephones are tested; transistorised
repeaters for submarine cables are being improved to give
them a life-span of at least twenty years.

According to 'Telecommunications Journal', within the
next 60 years the number of telephones in Britain will have
increased five-fold, and the number of calls may reach ten
times today's figure of 15,000,000 a day. Telephone services
will be built into houses, just as water, gas and electricity
are. There will be television telephones, with which you will
be able to see your caller and computers will revolutionise
the telecommunication services. The GPO foresee homes
with telephones all over the house, not merely one in the
hall; such homes will have an intercom system, and perhaps
a mobile telephone installed in the car, so that the subscriber
will be able to phone his business office or home whilst driving.
Gone will be the ugly TV aerials we see on nearly every roof
and chimney; such aerials that remain may be community
ones receiving broadcasts direct from satellites.

*The telephone kiosk on
the left was designed in
1935. As part of the GPO's
plans for modernization it
is being replaced by the
new design on the right.
The new kiosk has three
large panes of toughened
glass and a fibre-glass
roof which glows red when
the fluorescent lighting
inside is switched on*

ACKNOWLEDGMENTS

The author is greatly indebted to the General Post Office, and the *Telecommunications Journal* for their help with information and pictures in compiling this book. Thanks are due to the many Post Office Engineers who patiently explained the workings of telecommunication, and to Mr A. O. Milne for checking the manuscript; to Standard Telephone Cables Ltd for providing pictures and information; to the editor of *Soviet Weekly* for pictures and facts about the Moscow Tower; to Radio Stuttgart for information about their Tower; and to the United States Information Service Press Office for pictures and facts about satellites.

Bass line and tool kit holder

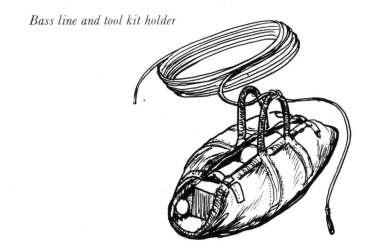

INDEX

A

aerials   9, 15, *16*, 17, 56, *57*, 58, 60
Alert   31
APT satellite   *54*
Ariel   31
ATS   56

B

BBC   8, 15
Birmingham post office tower   *19*

C

cables   12, 14, 16, 17, *18*, 21, 23, 24–34, *26, 27*
cable ships   *31*, 32–34, *33*
CANTAT   32
coastal radio stations   47–48, *48*
COMPAC   32

D

Datel   46
ducts   27

E

Echo   51
Estaunié, M   24

G

Goliath   29
Goonhilly   17, 56, *57*, 58
GRACE   41

I

Iris   31, 32
ITA   15

M

maser   58
Meteorological Office   17
microwaves   8–9, 16, 17, 20–23, 32, 49, 59
mole plough   *27*
Monarch   32, *33, 34*
Morse code   30
Moscow television tower   *22*, 49

N

NASA   50, 54, 56
National Physical Laboratory   11

O

Ostersund microwave tower   20

P

phonogram   44
Post Office Tower, London
   frontis,   8–20, *8, 10, 11*

R

Radar   17
radio   *18*, 23, 49, 51
radio beams   *8–9*, 17, 47–49
Relay   53, *53*
repeaters   28, *30*, 30–31, *33*, 49, 60

S

'Satellite Club'   23
satellites   17, 23, 49–59, *52, 53, 54, 55, 56*, 60
satellite tracking stations   56–59, *57*
Score   51

INDEX *Continued*

STD 41
Stuttgart radio tower *19, 21*
submarine cables 29–34, *30*, 60
SYNCOM *54*

T

telegram 43–44, *44*
telegraph 23, 24, 26
telephone 8, 13, 16, 17, 20, 26,
 35–43, 47, 49, 51, 52, 53, 59, *60*,
 60, *61*
telephone exchange 37–39

telephotos 52
teleprinter *45*, 44–46, 47
television 8, 14–15, 17, 20, 23,
 26, 49, 52, 53, 54, 55, 60
telex 44–46
Telstar *52*, 52, 56
TIM 15
transistors 29, *59*

W

waveguides 17, *18*

Earth station in Sweden

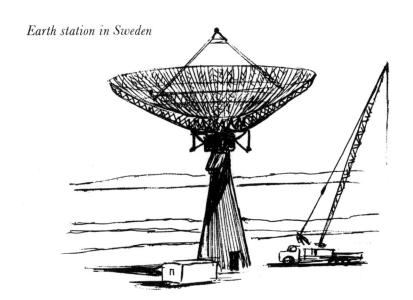